ABOUT US

We are a family of 4 travel enthusiasts & adventurers who want to share our knowledge with you in our ultimate itineraries & travel guides. We receive many questions from travelers looking for advice and insights about the countries we visit, so we created this itinerary to help you plan your dream vacation.

In 2018 we left our jobs and schools behind to travel the world and document our experiences on YouTube. We then packed up our things and moved to the beautiful Vancouver Island where we spend our time exploring and sharing our experiences online.

This ***Ultimate Whistler Travel Guide*** is for active families who want to pack in as much outdoor adventure as possible on their vacation!

LET'S CONNECT!

Email:
ContactUs@adventurecampitelli.com
www.adventurecampitelli.com

CONTENTS

Let's go to Whistler, BC!

Whistler, BC. is located in the Coast Mountains for British Columbia and is just a two hour drive North of Vancouver. It has one of the biggest ski resorts in North America and played host to the 2010 Winter Olympics in Vancouver. Whistler's stunning landscape includes glacier fed lakes, old growth forest, waterfalls, parks and paved trails perfect for walking or biking. Although mostly known as a ski destination, Whistler is also amazing in the summer.!

The stunning Whistler Village filled with accommodations, restaurants and shopping is located at the base of Whistler and Blackcomb Mountains and is the base for all your activities. You will fall in love with this place like we have!

Welcome to our Ultimate Whistler Summer Travel Guide! In this customizable travel planner and itinerary, you'll find amazing family activities to do from hiking and mountain biking to river jet boating and much more. Whether you're staying a few days or a couple of weeks, our suggested activities will help you plan your ideal vacation.

Also included in this travel planner is a general overview of accommodations, and a few of our favorite coffee shops and places to eat!

Download our free itinerary template at **www.adventurecampitelli.com/shop**

LET'S CONNECT!
Email: ContactUs @adventurecampitelli.com
www.adventurecampitelli.com

WHAT TO KNOW BEFORE YOU GO

BEFORE YOU PACK YOUR BAGS!

KNOW...

The current rules for entering Canada & the re-entry rules for your own country.

This information can be found on the government websites for Canada and your own country. The website **https://travel.gc.ca/** *has lots of good information.*

KNOW...

What vaccinations are required and recommended.

Rules are always changing so it's a good idea to double check before you leave for your trip.

KNOW...

Where the local hospitals and health clinics are. We've had to visit local hospitals a few times for minor things like stitches.

This is helpful to have written down in case someone falls ill or needs a stitch or two. The emergency number in Canada is **911***.*

KNOW...

What travel insurance is required including health insurance.

Let your insurance company know what activities you will be participating in to see if extra travel insurance is required.

Sample Itinerary

This sample itinerary is an idea of how you can plan your vacation. All of the activities written about in this planner are not covered in this itinerary.

- **Day 1:** Whistler Mountain Bike Park

- **Day 2:** Peak 2 Peak Gondola + Vallea Lumina

- **Day 3**: Ancient Cedars Trail hike + Scandinave Spa

- **Day 4:** Jet boating + Cycle the Valley Trail to 3 lakes

- **Day 5**: Train Wreck Trail hike + Paddle board at Alpha Lake

- **Day 6:** Ziplining + Rainbow Falls or chill at Lost Lake

- **Day 7:** Brandywine Falls - hope you enjoyed your Whistler vacation!

WHERE TO STAY

There are plenty of types of accommodations in Whistler including campgrounds, hostels with family rooms, hotels, condos, townhomes and luxury homes, many of which are listed on AirBnB. What you choose depends on your needs and budget. Our family typically books AirBnBs in places that have a kitchen to cook meals. Places that have a pool, hot tub and good bike storage also rank high on our list.

HOW TO GET AROUND

The best option by far is renting a car if it fits in your budget. A vehicle makes it easier to get to many activities listed in this guide.

Whistler is a very friendly walking and biking community with pathways connecting to most of Whistler's popular destinations. Other options include taxis, public transportation and free shuttle buses, making it possible to get around without having a car.

Below is a link with information about getting to and around Whistler. This includes public transit, Whistler Park Shuttles, links to trail maps, parking information and options on getting to Whistler.

https://www.whistler.ca/services/transportation/getting-to-and-around-whistler
Here is a direct link to the Whistler Transit System page: https://bctransit.com/whistler

WHERE TO EAT

There are a few grocery markets and pharmacies right in Whistler Village including the Whistler Grocery Store, Fresh St. Market and Upper Village Market. The Whistler app lists all of the grocery stores. A few of our favorite spots to eat and grab coffee include:

- Moguls cafe – by far our favorite place for lattes!
- Ecology coffee – clothing store and coffee shop in one.
- Purebread – amazing baked goods. Worth lining up for!
- La Cantina – tacos, burritos and more. A fun vibe!
- Pizzeria Antico – delicious Neapolitan pizza place. Great atmosphere.
- Creekbread – organic wood-fired pizza. Delicious.

Top 3 Must Have Apps

These three apps will make your active vacation in Whistler smoother by assisting with navigation while driving and on the trails, as well as an app that covers almost everything about Whistler.

Download Before You Leave

Google Maps

This works well in Whistler for all of your navigation.

All Trails

An app used for outdoor activities including hiking and mountain biking. Provides detailed maps of trails.

Whistler

A really good app for everything Whistler!

WHISTLER VILLAGE ACTIVITIES

Whistler Village is the heart and soul of the town of Whistler. It is a year round resort that is bustling with activity during the summer months. It's a welcoming place and tourists flock here from all over the world, making it a destination you'll never forget.

From a range of spectacular accommodations, shopping and dining, to the Whistler Mountain Bike Park, Peak 2 Peak Gondola and endless hiking trails, this is where your adventure begins.

This section covers fun summer activities that occur right within the Village. It's a playground for adults and kids alike!

Whistler Village

Whistler Mountain Bike Park

- This bike park is the number one lift-accessed bike park in the world with more than 1501 verticle metres (4926 feet) and over 80km (50mi) covering 112 trails. This magnificent park is accessible for all skill levels from easy green runs to double black and pro-level trails. We've seen all ages here from as young as 5 to well in their 70's.

- As of 2021, a 1 day Adult day pass costs $83CDN ($66USD), $75 CDN ($59USD) for teens ages 13-18 and $48CDN ($38USD) for kids ages 5-12. If you plan to ride more than one day, we suggest you purchase a multi-day pass (2-5 day options).

- There are many bike and equipment rental shops as well as lessons for all ages and day camps for kids. Our daughter (who was 10 at the time), did a one day DFX lesson and had an amazing time!

- Check out the website for more information: www.whistlerblackcomb.com

- If the kids are biking for the day, it's the perfect chance for some adult time!

Whistler Village
Peak 2 Peak Gondola

- Connects the top of Whistler and Blackcomb mountains. 3 fun facts:
  - 1. Longest unsupported span between two cable car towers at 3 km (1.88mi).
  - 2. Highest cable car above ground at 436 metres (1430 feet).
  - 3. Longest continuous lift system.

- You access the Peak 2 Peak by purchasing a 360 Experience ticket either online (https://www.whistler.com/activities/peak-to-peak-gondola) or at any ticket booth at the base of the village. In the summer, you can only reach the Peak 2 Peak gondola by taking the chairlift from the Upper Village at Blackcomb Mountain. The cost is $78 CDN ($62USD) per adult, $69 CDN ($54USD) per youth, and $40 CDN ($32USD) per child.

- The silver gondolas have a glass section on the bottom for a cool view of the valley below. There are fewer of these gondolas making the wait time longer. Take the red Gondola out and the silver one back.

- The 360 degree Experience ticket gives you access to the Blackcomb chair to get to the Peak 2 Peak Gondola, access to the Gondola, access to the Peak Express chair lift that takes you to The Cloudraker Skybridge and The Raven's Eye viewing platform. Kids under 1metre (3.3 feet) are not able to go on the Peak Express chair.

- If you can, taking the Peak Express chair lift to the Cloudraker Skybridge, a 130 metre (426.5 feet) suspension bridge for a really cool experience.

- There are lots of hiking trails at the top to explore. Stop off at the RoundHouse Lodge for some well deserved food and drinks!

Whistler Village

Whistler Skate Park

- Whistler has the second largest skate park in Canada, with over 4600 square metres (50,000 square feet) of skating space. The park is located between Whistler Village and Fitzsimmons Creek, just a few minutes away from Whistler Village. It's loaded with many fun features including a "Snake bowl", ¼ pipes up to 3 metres (3 feet), a spine, volcano, central pyramid, and long flowly lines with multiple ledges.

- Lights stay on until 1 a.m!

Fitzsimmons Creek Bike Skills Park

- Located along Valley Trail, a couple minutes south of the Skate Park is the Fitzsimmons Creek bike skills park. This skills park has a lot of fun features to improve one's bike skills including a jump track, pump track, beginner and intermediate skills area.

- This is a great spot for kids to practice their skills and it's free!

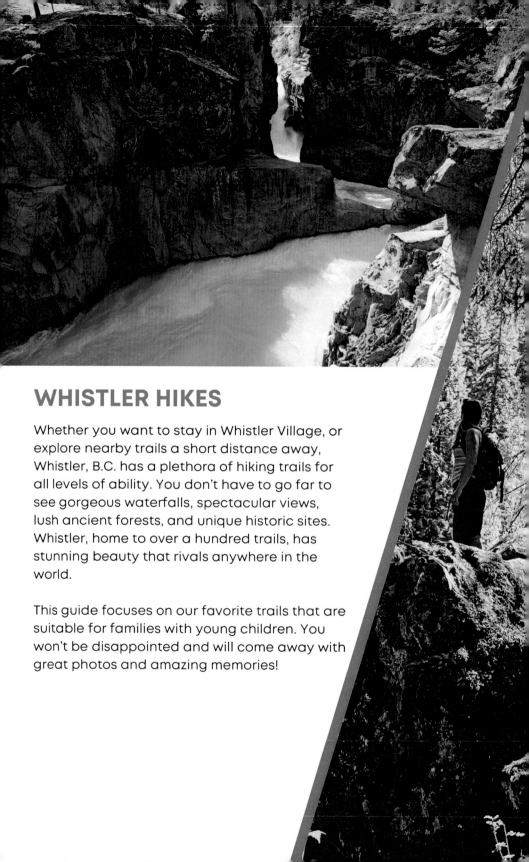

WHISTLER HIKES

Whether you want to stay in Whistler Village, or explore nearby trails a short distance away, Whistler, B.C. has a plethora of hiking trails for all levels of ability. You don't have to go far to see gorgeous waterfalls, spectacular views, lush ancient forests, and unique historic sites. Whistler, home to over a hundred trails, has stunning beauty that rivals anywhere in the world.

This guide focuses on our favorite trails that are suitable for families with young children. You won't be disappointed and will come away with great photos and amazing memories!

Whistler Hikes

Trainwreck Trail

- This short 2.3km (1.4mi) trail is one of Whistler's most unique spots and a favorite with hikers, mountain bikers, photographers and graffiti artists.

- This hidden gem of a hike leads you to old train boxcars strewn in the middle of the forest amongst tall cedar and fir trees near the Cheakamus River.

- This hike used to be illegal to get to because you had to access the site by walking along the train tracks. Now there's a suspension bridge crossing the river giving easy access to this cool historical site.

- The story of how the boxcars ended up there was that it derailed in 1956 when the train, going way over the speed limit in an area under repair, had the fourth engine leave the tracks causing the crash. Three cars apparently got wedged into a canyon and eventually were dragged back up into the forest, where they remain.

- They are spray painted with graffiti art that really adds to the uniqueness of the site.

- From Whistler Village, it's about a 12 minute drive to the parking lot for the trail. Parking is located at the Interpretive Forest off Cheakamus Lake Road on the east side of highway 99.

- **Time:** It takes less than 30 minutes to get to the train wreck but you'll want extra time to explore the boxcars and take some photos. Plan for about 2 hours total here.

Whistler Hikes

Nairn Falls

- To get to Nairn Falls drive north along the Sea to Sky Highway (Highway 99) for about 25 minutes to the parking lot. and is between Whistler and Pemberton.

- This short 2.6km (1.6mi) out and back hike along the stunning Green River, leads you to two viewing platforms overlooking the upper and lower falls, each about 30 metres (98 feet). This waterfall is quite powerfull and the hike is easy to do for the whole family.

- Starting right from the Nairn Falls Provincial parking lot, there is a day lot on the right as you enter the park. The trail starts near the washrooms at the edge of the parking lot and follows the river all the way along the gorgeous path to the waterfall.

- **Time:** This hike can easily be done in under an hour, although we spent quite a bit of time here taking photos.

- Not much planning is required to do this hike as it is easy to find and relatively short. You can easily add it on to another activity in the same area.

- There is a nice campground here as well.

Whistler Hikes

Brandywine Falls

- If you're short on time but would still like to take in an iconic waterfall, add Brandywine Falls to your itinerary. It is a beautiful 70 metre (230 foot) waterfall cascading over a wall of volcanic rocks.

- The 1km (0.6 mi) out and back trail is an easy, short walk with a spectacular reward for not much effort and arguably one of the nicest Whistler area waterfalls. Heading south for about 20 minutes on the Sea to Sky Highway from Whistler Village, the trail is on the east side of the highway.

- Starting from the parking lot, head over the wooden bridge, turn right and keep going until you reach the viewing platform. You'll cross some railroad tracks along the way. You won't be disappointed!

- **Time:** You could do this in about an hour including drive times.

Whistler Hikes

Rainbow Falls

- Rainbow Falls trailhead is just a 15 minute drive north from Whistler Village and a fairly short hike along Twenty One Mile Creek. The parking area is along Alta Lake Road where you'll find a wooden map board located at the trail called Rainbow Hiking Trail outlining the route. This same trailhead also accesses other trails including Rainbow Lake, Hanging Lake and Madeley lake.

- Follow the trail immediately heading up and look for a sign marking the way to Rainbow Falls which will be to the right. Follow the trail and you will hear the sound of the roaring falls. After seeing the falls, you will walk back up to the main trail and return to the parking the same direction you came or head up the trail and loop back and down the other side. The loop is 2.2km (1.3mi) and rated as an easy trail.

- **Time:** Plan for 1.5-2 hours.

Whistler Hikes

Ancient Cedars Hike

- This trail leads to some of the biggest, oldest and most beautiful trees in the Whistler Valley. This trail, north of Whistler, is home to 900 + year old Cedar trees, a beautiful mossy forest bed, a couple of stunning views and a small water fall.

- The trail is about 10km (6.2 mi) north of Whistler, just past Green Lake with a left onto Cougar Mountain Road. A car is required to access the trailhead heading up a bumpy logging road to the parking area. A 4x4 is recommended for the clearance but not a must. The drive takes about 20 minutes from Whistler Village.

- The 5km (3.1mi) fairly easy hike is well marked with signs and posts. Be sure to check out the viewpoints along the way for a scenic look onto the valley. The path will lead to a pretty waterfall below the wooden bridge and then take you on a loop through the old cedar trees. Lots of great photo opportunities here and a good hike for all ages! Anyone want to hug a 900 year old tree?

- **Expert tip:** Bring lots of water and snacks. It can get quite hot on the trail in the summer.

- **Time:** Plan for about 3-4 hours.

Whistler Hikes

Parkhurst Ghost Town

- Parkhurst was a logging town near Green Lake that was founded in the 1920s and abandoned in the 1960s. Historical artifacts still remain such as an intact cabin, flattened buildings, abandoned vehicles and even an old stove.

- It is a tricky trail to find and navigate so make sure you have **AllTrails app** downloaded. This 7.7km (4.8mi) loop is an easy trail and can be done by either hiking our mountain biking. We chose to mountain bike so we could get to the town more quickly.

- To get there, drive North on the Sea to Sky Highway past the end of Green lake for about 10km (6.2mi). Follow the signs for Wedgemount Lake trail and turn right onto Wedge Creek Forest Service Road taking the single lane bridge over the Green River. On the other side turn right and drive past the turn off for Whistler Paintball. After the road passes two locked yellow gates on the left, pull over and park.

- From the trailhead, you follow the gravel road behind the second yellow gate and follow the Sea to Sky trail signs on this section. After crossing a wood bridge over the creek, stay on the road and follow the hairpin turn. You will end up on single track for Sea to Sky trail. This is where we had to pull out AllTrails quite often as the trail isn't well marked. There are orange ribbons on the trees marking the trail so you can follow these as well. Once you get there, a small loop takes you around the town and meets up with the trail you came in on. You can either go back the way you came or take the loop taking Parkhurst trail back to the car.

Parkhurst Ghost Town

- Another way to see the town would be to park at Green Lake Park near the boat launch and paddle over by kayak, paddle board or canoe.

- **Time:** Plan to spend 2 hours if you are biking and likely 3-4 hours if hiking.

- **Expert Tip:** Bring bear spray and make lots of noise.

- One of the coolest hikes here!

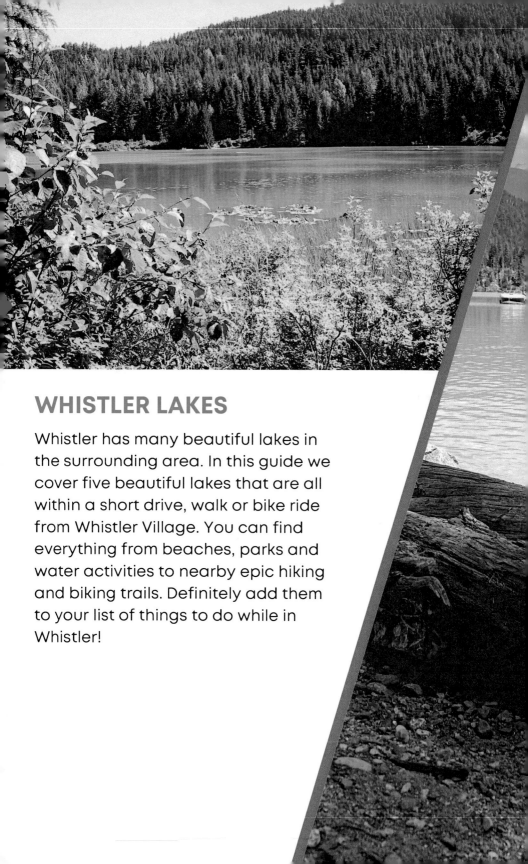

WHISTLER LAKES

Whistler has many beautiful lakes in the surrounding area. In this guide we cover five beautiful lakes that are all within a short drive, walk or bike ride from Whistler Village. You can find everything from beaches, parks and water activities to nearby epic hiking and biking trails. Definitely add them to your list of things to do while in Whistler!

WHISTLER LAKES

Valley Trail bike ride to Alta lake, Nita Lake and Alpha Lake

- The Valley Trail in Whistler is a large 45km (28mi) pathway system connects Whistler neighborhoods including Whistler Village, lakes and various viewpoints. It connects to the Sea to Sky Trail that is part of the Trans Canada Trai. The pathway is well maintained and makes for a fun, scenic and relaxing day around three beautiful lakes. Cycling to the three lakes is about a 10.4km (6.5mi) out and back trip. The pathway continues on further if you're looking for a longer ride. We absolutely loved this ride!

- **Time:** Plan for 3-4 hours including time at the lakes.

Helpful Facts:

Bike Valet

- Rainbow Park at Alta Lake offers a valet service for bikes on Fridays, Saturdays and Sundays during the summer if you want to cycle there and not have to worry about your bikes being stolen while enjoying water activities. Visit www.whistler.ca/BikeParking to find out more.

Park Eats

- Many Whistler Parks including Alpha Lake Park, Lakeside Park and Rainbow Park have pop-vendor services, delivery and food trucks during the summer. Food includes crepes, gelato, pizza, burgers, sandwiches, salads and other offerings.

Free Shuttle

- A free shuttle going to Rainbow Park is offered during the summer months on the weekends from 10am-6pm. Large items like un-inflatable water toys, food coolers and fold up chairs are allowed.

WHISTLER LAKES

Valley Trail bike ride to Alta lake, Nita lake and Alpha lake

Alta Lake

- This is the biggest and warmest lake in Whistler and perfect for swimming. There are 3 beaches at this lake including Rainbow park, Lakeside Park and Alta Park.

- Rainbow Park, on the west side of the lake, is the largest park and has a lot of activities including numerous volleyball fields as well as a dog beach. Other amenities include washrooms, a concession stand that rents canoes and kayaks, picnic tables and barbeques. It's about a 12 minute bike ride from Whistler Village and more of a destination if you are planning to stay there for at least of a couple of hours.

- Lakeside park is along the Valley trail cycling route making it a nice stopping point along the way. It is a short 10 minute bike ride from Whistler Village. There is a large grassy section, a sandy beach, picnic tables, barbeques, washrooms and a concession stand that rents canoes and kayaks.

Nita Lake

- Heading southwest along Valley Trail another 3.5km (2mi) from Lakeside Park, you'll come to Nita Lake. A small relaxing late with Nita Lake Lodge along it's shore, it has a small gravel beach with a creek flowing through it. This creek is known for fishing and has a couple of picnic tables nearby.

Alpha Lake

- Continuing along the path from Nita Lake, you'll come to Alpha Lake, bearing its name from the first letter of the Greek Alphabet. This lake has a large grassy area, dock, volleyball court, kids playground and a small sandy area at Alpha Lake Park. This is a nice place to spend some time and a great lake for paddle boarding!

WHISTLER LAKES

Green Lake

- Green Lake is a beautiful aqua colored glacier fed lake that is an easy walk or bike ride from Whistler Village. This is the largest and deepest of Whistler's lakes and it is quite cold to swim in. Green Lake is the local airport for Harbour Air Seaplanes.

- If you ride or walk north along Valley Trail from Whistler Village, you'll reach a nice wooden boardwalk that wraps part way around Green Lake. Along the route you will pass through Dream River Park and past Harbour Air to Fitzsimmons Fan Park. This path will take you to "The Spit", a sandbar from the edge of Green lake that juts out into the water. It's a great spot to watch the seaplanes take off and land!

- Another option is to visit Green Lake Park, a small park on the North side of the lake next to a cul-de-sac of lakefront houses. This park is about a ten minute drive North from Whistler Village, located just off the Sea to Sky highway on Lakeshore Drive. This tiny park has washrooms, picnic tables and a small rocky beach that is great to kayak or paddle board from. If you want to visit Parkhurst Ghost Town by paddle board or kayak, this would be a good spot to launch from. If you follow Lakeshore drive around to the left, there is another little spot down a narrow road that you can park at. It has a dock and is a nice spot to take in the view of the lake.

Lost Lake

- This pretty lake is short 20 minute walk or 5 minute bike ride from Whistler Village. It is a great spot for swimming with a nice grassy area, a beach with a pier and a few floating rafts that you swim up to and jump off. There are washroom facilities and picnic tables. Grab a snack or lunch from the food trucks that park here in the summer.

- Dogs aren't allowed at Lost Lake Park beach but if you walk part way around the lake, you'll come to Canine Cove, a beach that allows dogs.

- There is a 5km (3.1mi) easy gravel trail called Lost lake loop that goes all the way around the lake for biking or walking. Lots of hiking and mountain biking trails are in this area as a part of the Lost Lake trail system so go exploring!

OTHER AWESOME ACTIVITIES

When people think of Whistler, images of skiing and mountain biking come to mind but there are so many more activities to do in this adventurous mountain paradise.

In this section, we cover a mix of fun and exciting options to add to your itinerary.

OTHER AWESOME ACTIVITIES

Whistler Jet Boating

- Have you ever gone jet boating on a river? Probably not! This thrilling tour takes you up the Green River to the base of Nairn Falls. Out in the backcountry, you are guided through white rapids with stunning scenery of old growth forests and high mountain peaks.

- The captain is highly skilled weaving the boat in and around trees, large rocks and river swells while providing an interesting commentary about the area. Due to being a protected wetland area, Whistler Jet Boating is the only company that is allowed to provide the river tours.

- The price is $119CDN ($93USD) per adult and $99CDN ($78USD) for kids and youth. The tour lasts one hour and departure times are 9am, 12pm and 3pm daily from May to September.

- Our kids absolutely loved this activity!

- Website: https://www.whistlerjetboating.com/

- Head north on the Sea to Sky Highway for about 35 minutes to Pemberton. Turn on airport road towards Sunstone Golf Club Bar & Grill and park in the parking lot. This is where you meet your guide.

- **Time:** Plan for about 2.5 hours for this activity including drive time.

OTHER AWESOME ACTIVITIES

Vallea Lumina

- This is a unique experience you have got to do! It's a multimedia night walk/hike in the middle of the forest with thousands of lights and music taking you on an immersive experience following a story of two lost hikers from the 1900's. The use of holograms was phenomenal and the show was far better than we expected. It brings the forest to life and really makes you feel a part of the story. There is a concession stand, fires and places to sit at the entrance/exit making it a nice way to end the evening.

- The cost is about $35CDN ($28USD) for adults and $30CDN ($24USD) for youth ages 6-15. You must bookyour tickets online: http://www.vallealumina.com/

- Vallea Lumina takes place at night (once the sun has gone down) Cougar Mountain, a 15 minute drive north along the Sea to Sky highway to Courgar Mountain Road. Check the website for information about their shuttle service if you would like this option.

- **Time:** The well lit pathway is 1.5km long and takes about 50-80 minutes to complete. It is a forested hiking trail but not difficult. Allow 2-2.5 hours including the drive.

OTHER AWESOME ACTIVITIES
White Water Rafting

- White water rafting is always a fun adventure for our family. There are a few white water rafting companies in Whistler so do your research to see what is the best fit for your family.

- Rafting occurs on several rivers in the Whistler area including the Green River, Lower Cheakamus, Elaho and Squamish Rivers. All have different classes of rapids ranging from 1-2 to 3-4 rapids. The one thing about white water rafting in Whistler is that the scenery is beautiful!

- Prices start around $110CDN ($87 USD) per adult and $75CDN ($59USD) for kids ages 5-16. Of course, this depends on the company and the tour you choose.

- Canadian Outback Rafting Company has a good tour for families with little kids (minimum age is 5). See www.raftwhistler.com

- **Time:** Plan for 3-4 hours depending on the tour.

OTHER AWESOME ACTIVITIES

Ziplining

- If you haven't gone ziplining before, Whistler is a great place to go! It is a good place to get over your fear of heights and kids as young as 6 can participate. There are a couple of companies that operate out of Whistler and they have different tours available. The Ziptrek Company has a few different tours including the longest zipline in all of North America. This one is sold as a separate experience from the other zipline tours it offers.

- Superfly Ziplines has one tour but their ziplines are side by side so you go at the same time as another person which is cool. The minimum age here is 7.

- Don't worry, you get instruction and practice on how to safely use the ziplines prior to going on the zipline courses.

Tour operators:
- https://superflyziplines.com/ziplines/
- https://whistler.ziptrek.com/

- Prices start at $140CDN ($111USD) per adult and $120CDN ($95USD) per kid.

- **Time:** Plan for about 3 hours for this activity (depending on the tour).

OTHER AWESOME ACTIVITIES

Whistler Tree Adventure Tours

- Have you ever done a high ropes course? Tightropes, planks, swinging logs, ziplines, ladders and high bridges challenge your strength, balance and agility and is a super fun family activity.

- At Whistler Tree Adventure Tours there are obstacle courses for all ages (starting at age 7) and all abilities from beginner to advanced. I have a bit of a fear of heights so an activity like this helps to conquer those fears. If you're like me, high ropes beginner courses are totally doable. Wearing a safety harness and clipping in at every station also provides you the confidence to challenge yourself and reach new limits!

- Prices start at about $60CDN ($47 USD) per adult and $55CDN ($43USD) per kid, depending on which tour that you do. This activity takes place at the Superfly Ziplines Basecamp on Cougar Mountain, a 15 minute drive North on the Sea to Sky Highway and then left onto Cougar Mountain Road.

- **Time:** Duration is anywhere from 1.5 to 4.5 hours depending on which course you do.

- **Expert Tip:** If you have them, where fingerless athletic gloves to help with grip and keep your hands from getting blistered.

OTHER AWESOME ACTIVITIES

Whistler ATV Tours

- Although not really active, ATV tours can be fun and exhilarating. ATV's allow you access to backcountry that may be difficult to get to plus you can cover more distance taking in more nature. You must be 19 and older with a valid driver's license to operate the ATV but you can take a child passenger.

- There are several tours available and prices start at $149 CDN ($118 USD) per adult.

- Another cool tour offered is called the Side X Side UTV tours where you sit in a two-person all terrain vehicle that looks like dune buggy. Again, drivers must be over the age of 19 with a valid driver's license.

- Visit the Whistler tourism site for more information: www.whistler.com/activities/atv

Whistler Golf

- Whistler is rated as British Columbia's number one golf destination boasting four championship designer golf courses. They offer group packages and lots of people flock to Whistler for their golf vacation getaways.

- **Visit:** https://www.golfwhistler.com/

Whistler Relax

This beautiful Spa this is worth a visit!

Scandinave Spa

If you're looking for an adult afternoon to relax, and get away from it all then check out this spa! With traditional Scandinavian open-air hot and cold baths in a beautiful natural setting, you can soak away your sore muscles and relax. Hint: sign them up for a day camp and to get that much needed time away.

You can reserve a booking to use just the baths or you can pair it with a massage.

Prices for the baths are $130 CDN ($103 USD) during the week and $145 CDN ($115 USD) on the weekends. Prices for massages vary.

Website: https://www.scandinave.com/whistler/en/

The spa is located a 5 minutes drive north of Whistler Village.

Disclaimer

The information provided in this itinerary is based on our experiences and research. All costs and activities are up to date as per the publication date of this itinerary and subject to change. Always do your own research, check government websites for latest travel information and choose activities based on your interests, comfort level and ability.

Published February, 2022

Visit our YouTube channel!
@AdventureCampitelli

Whistler is one of our favorite places to visit. Check out our YouTube channel to watch our Whistler videos.

https://www.youtube.com/adventurecampitelli

Whistler: 5 family summer activities
- ***https://youtu.be/RolRmTL9CfE***

Whistler: 7 more summer activities
- ***https://youtu.be/mEJhW-rAxNQ***

What's your
adventure?

Made in United States
North Haven, CT
28 July 2022

21963901R00020